1

The Entered Apprentice Handbook

By

J.S.M. Ward

Circa 1920's

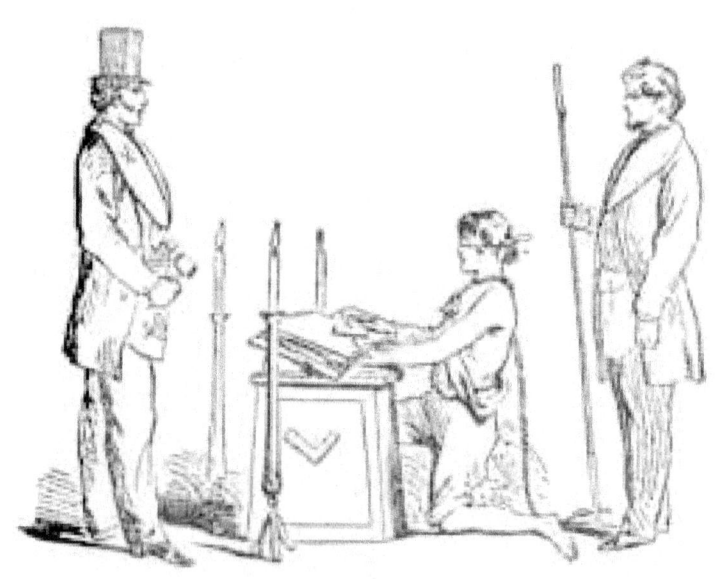

The Entered Apprentice Handbook

By
J.S.M. Ward

INTRODUCTION
By The Hon. SIR John A. Cockburn

W. Bro. Ward is one of the most able and earnest of Masonic students. He brings to bear on the task of research the mind of a scholar, enriched by extensive reading, much travel and a wide experience of men and affairs. In addition to being a well-known author of Masonic Works, he was the Founder of the Masonic Study Society, whose first President was the late Sir Richard Vassar Vassar-Smith, 33 degree, and in whose ranks are to be found many eminent Masonic writers. Brother Ward has by precept and example led others to become eager explorers in the realmsof Masonic truth. The present volume is No. 1 in a series of studies as to the meaning of our Ritual. It deals with the degree of an Entered Apprentice and is calculated to inspire the younger brethren with the resolve not to content themselves with the outward form of our ceremonies, beautiful though it be, but to gain a knowledge of the indwelling soul of Masonry and to comprehend the deep meaning of the ritual with which they are step by step becoming familiar. Hence they will learn to regard the Craft not only as a world-spread, civilizing medium, nor yet only as the most benevolent of all Institutions, but also as a mine of surpassing wealth in which the Wisdom of the Ages has become embedded and preserved. Bro. Ward at the outset disarms anything like hostile criticism by admitting that many brethren may not find themselves in complete accord with all his conclusions. Indeed, it would be surprising if this were the case. Like Holy Writ, the Ritual is capable of many interpretations. It is a gradual accretion in which succeeding epochs have left their mark. Evolution takes place under the alternation of forces that make for difference and agreement. The process demands a continual adjustment between these apparently contrary, but in reality complementary factors. Each age sets out to balance any deficiency in the preceding period. When materialism has been pushed to excess, the tendency is rectified by a spiritual revival. On the other hand, an age in which zeal for the gifts of the spirit has caused neglect of temporal welfare is naturally followed by a renaissance of the just claims of the flesh. The subject matter of Masonry is the relationship between Spirit and Matter, between Heaven and Earth, between God and Man, between the Soul and the Body. Emphasis is everywhere laid on the necessity of their reconciliation. Consequently to attain the just milieu emphasis has sometimes to be laid on one side and sometimes on the other. For example, the Cross and the Square, which have now such deeply spiritual significance , were originally signs of Earth, and became respectively, the essential symbols of Christianity and Masonry, because it was necessary to proclaim the fact that professions of piety towards God were idle, unless they bore fruit in kindly relationship between man and man. Bro. Ward regards the J.W. as representing the body, and the S.W. the soul, although the emblems and jewel of the former are celestial and of the latter terrestrial. The fact is that things divine and human are so interwoven in Masonry as to be inseparable. Duty towards God and towards our neighbor are but different aspects of the same truth. For the

Fatherhood of God implies the Brotherhood of Man, and, conversely, he who devotes himself to the service of his fellow creatures proves, through his brotherly relationship, his descent from the Father of All. The issue of Bro. Ward's series of handbooks cannot fail to accomplish its main object, which is to lead not only juniors, but also those well versed in the ritual, to mark, learn and inwardly digest the significance of the ceremonies, which when properly understood, causes our jewels and emblems to glow with an inner light which infinitely enhances their beauty. The ready reception which Bro. Ward's books have already received at the hands of the Craft, prove that they meet a recognized requirement as expositions of the character of a ritual with whose external features we are familiar, and in which we take our daily delight.

J.A.C.

The Mysteries

In every race and every clime,
Since the earliest days of Time,
Men have taught the Mystic Quest Shown the Way
to Peace and rest.

Bacchus died, and rose again,
On the golden Asian Plain;
Osiris rose from out the grave, And thereby mankind
did save:
Adonis likewise shed his blood
By the yellow Syrian flood,
Zoroaster brought to birth
Mithra from His Cave of Earth.

And to-day in Christian Lands We with them can
join hands.

J.W.

CHAPTER I.
THE OPENING OF THE FIRST DEGREE.

The W.M. calls the brethren together with one knock so as to remind them that the body must be prepared to obey the higher faculties, for if it is not, no spiritual progress is possible. The first question and answer of the J.W. indicate this quite clearly, for the J.W. represents the body and so he satisfies himself that man's body is on guard against outside influences.

The S.W., representing the Soul, next proves that all present have made some progress towards the light. It is only when this has been achieved that any real advancement becomes possible, and only those who have started can help those who still remain in spiritual darkness.

The next series of questions indicates that Man has a seven-fold nature.

The Ancient Egyptians held this view , and it is endorsed in Masonry by the fact that it takes seven to make a perfect lodge. There is also, no doubt, an astrological reference to the seven planets and a connection with stellar worship, but as our system is mainly solar, it is almost impossible to give a logical planetary interpretation to the seven who form a lodge, or to the seven officers. In short, the planetary symbolism has become disorganized by the stress laid on the solar aspect of the three principal officers who rule a lodge. Moreover, the predominance of the solar aspect has emphasized the triune nature of man, and symbolizes it in these officers.

Thus it will be seen that too much stress must not be laid on the planets, as represented by the seven officers, and a passing reference to the fact that it is still remembered in the number seven is all that can be logically maintained.

Similarly there is merely a hint of the seven-fold nature of man. If ours were a stellar system, then clearly the Tyler would represent the body, the divine spark would be represented by the W.M. , the various officers between would symbolize the various subdivisions of the non-materials parts of man, such as his astral body, his intellectual faculties, and so forth.

Since, however, our system is solar in the main, we should continue to interpret our symbols from that aspect, making but passing reference to stellar influences when they occur.

The duties of the Tyler are considered elsewhere, so we will pass to the I.G. Although in some popular workings he and the other two subordinate officers are not allowed to speak for themselves, the Wardens doing this work, in many other rituals they are allowed to answer the W.M. direct.

The I.G. stands for the power which permits the Soul to enter flesh at any given moment. The Soul may desire to become incarnate, but unless its time has come it is turned back at the threshold, and even if it forces itself into birth it is cut short. Entry into life is not an accident, but ordained of God, Who works through His spiritual as well as through His human agents.

Those who saw Maeterlinck's play, "The Blue Bird," will remember that the same idea is dealt with in one of the scenes.

Spiritually, the I.G. represents the warning which must be given to those who attempt, without due caution, to probe into the Mysteries of God. They must neither rush forward hastily, nor, having once started, withdraw suddenly; for, if they do, dire evil will befall.

This warning all the Mysteries gave, and it is certain that those who dabble in the so called occult run grave risks unless they use the utmost caution. Hence it is absolutely essential that the candidate should be properly prepared before he starts on his quest.

The J.D. represents the physical means by which the Soul, represented by the S.W., passes on the inspirations received from the Spirit, the W.M., to the material world. In this sense therefore he represents intelligence, and the five senses of man, whereas the S.D. stands for intuition, whereby the Soul obtains its inspiration from the Divine.

In the ancient operative days these officers no doubt had a practical use, the S.D. being the personal messenger of the Master, who took messages to the S.W., not merely when in Lodge, but when he was at a distance, employed on his task, or possibly when

he was resting from his labors, In like manner the
S.W. 's deacon was sent by him to find the J.W.

The J.W. describes his position in L. and indicates
quite clearly that he represents the Sun at noon.

From the operative point of view it must be
remembered that Noon has always been, and still is,
a workingman's dinner hour, hence the special duty
of the J.W. ; but in the spiritual sense, since he stands
for the body, it is natural that he should have charge
over the body's needs. As he also represents the
preservative side of God, his interest in the physical
well-being of man is appropriate. With this in mind
the F. C. will realize the significance of the P.W., and
its connection with C. and W. , which are the
emblems of the God of Vegetation in the more
primitive rites. When men evolved, and the solar
system of religion developed, the God of Vegetation
became the Preserver. This characteristic of the J.W.
is emphasized by the upright lines of his plumb,
which latter reminds us of water which falls from
heaven, and of the cast marks of Vishnu in India.

This aspect of the J.W., as representing the Preserver
, is carefully maintained throughout the whole of the
three degrees and must never be forgotten. In like
manner, the fact that he stands for the body is also
maintained throughout. Bearing this in mind, we
shall perceive the significance of the fact that the
Architect of K.S. 's Temple was the J.W.
Finally, bread and water represent the bare
necessities, without which mortal life cannot be
preserved. Luxuries, which are obtained when we

13

have acquired worldly possessions, i.e., wealth, lead to the death of the soul, and even of the body, unless employed with the greatest caution.

Some masons claim that the J.W. originally sat in the North to mark the Sun at noon, meaning to see, or point out, that it had reached the mid heavens. Honestly, I can find no real evidence in support of this view, which likewise places the W.M. in the West and the S.W. in the East.

It is due, in my opinion, to a complete misunderstanding of the use of the words "to mark." This phrase implies that the J.W. is placed on a certain spot to mark the position of the Sun at noon, and not that 'he may see it. In a closed-in building, such as a lodge room was, it would be desirable to mark the three positions of the Sun, for the candidate has to pass through each point in turn, and these three officers, who represent the Sun in its three aspects, would naturally sit in the positions in use in a speculative lodge.

Any arguments adduced from the rituals of the modern Operative Lodges are vitiated by two facts- (1) we have no evidence that this peculiarity is really old (it may be due to Stretton's inventive mind) and (2) the Operatives, if old, would be descended from the Guild Masons and not from the Freemasons; and this might be a peculiarity of theirs, or deliberately adopted so as to differentiate them from the Freemasons.

That the Guild Masons and Freemasons were quite distinct has been proved as far back as 1913, and the fact is gone into in my other book, "Freemasonry and the Ancient Gods." That the Operatives are not descended direct from the Mediaeval Freemasons is shown by the fact that they have entirely different signs from our own.

Thus we need not discuss further the question as to whether the J.W. should be in the North or South.

The S.W., as he indicates in his reply to the W.M., represents the Sun in its setting, and so the Destructive Side of the Deity, or Shiva. He also stands for the Soul. Shiva shall close not only our mortal life, but Time itself. But I have dealt with this side of the S.W. very fully elsewhere.

It should be noted, however, that the S.W. is associated with level and horizontal lines , and not with perpendiculars, and here again he follows the Hindoo system, for Shiva's caste mark is two or more parallel lines. As the Great Leveller this is most natural, and it reminds us that in the sight of God all souls are equal, even though in mortal life their stations may appear to differ.

Shiva is associated with the element of Fire, whereas Vishnu is associated with Water, and as we see that great care has been taken to maintain the connection between the J.W. and Water, so we find that with us the S.W. is similarly associated with Fire, though perhaps less obviously. Firstly, his level is of a triangular form with the point upward, the world-wide symbol for Fire. Again, the S.W. 's P.W. has hidden within it the same idea. A smith who works in metals can only do so by the help of fire, and in one ritual this fact is stressed. Thus metals come out from the dark earth, and the Sun sinks in the West into darkness and the grave, as does man.

But, by means of fire, man obtains wealth from the metals hidden in the earth, and in like manner the Soul of Man rises refined and purified from the grave by means of the divine fire within. Moreover, one cannot ignore the fact that there is here a hint of the necessity of the purging fire of remorse to cleanse away our sins.

The S. W. is the Soul, the link between mortal life and the Divine Spark , but he acts on instructions from the Spirit; in other words, it is only when God decrees our death that the Soul departs from the body.

The W.M. represents, as his words indicate, the creative side of God and the Divine Spirit in Man. He sets us to work on earth, but delegates to another the task of calling us back whence we came. He represents the male aspect of the Deity, as is shown by the tau crosses, called levels, on his apron, and by his use of the gavel, which represents the same emblem. The Tau Cross is, of course, a phallic symbol and stands for the male and creative aspect in Man.

As the three principal officers represent the Sun (a masculine planet) in various phases, it is natural that they should all wield the gavel, but the two wardens are less essentially male than the W.M., as is indicated by the fact that they do not have the tau cross or Master's level on their aprons. The Spirit, being active, is male; whereas both soul and body, being more or less passive, are female. The feminine side of the S.W. or Soul is deliberately emphasized later-in the first degree-by a reference to the Moon, a feminine planet, the emblem of the Soul and of the psychic nature in man. Nor can we ignore the fact that the West is known as the feminine quarter of the heavens, whereas the East is the masculine; it is also worth noticing that Shiva is often depicted with the moon.

Finally, before declaring the L. open, the W.M. offers up a prayer, thereby reminding us that the Divine Spark in Man, or the Spirit, must turn to the Source of All for aid if it would control body and soul.

The three knocks, as distinct from the one knock with which the proceedings started, indicate that the members are about to work for the union and advancement of body, soul and spirit, and not for the body only. But the way in which the three knocks are given show that, as yet, there is no unity between the three elements which constitute Man.

CHAPTER II.

17

THE TYLER

The first thing that greets the eyes of the aspirant to our Order is a man, whom he soon discovers is called the Tyler, standing in front of the door with a d.n. s.d. in his hand. He naturally wants an answer to the question which actually occurs in a certain famous old ritual, "Why does the Tyler wear a s.d.?"-and the answer is, "To guard the brethren and to hele the Word."

Let us consider this answer:-

"To guard the brethren. "In certain old rituals of the 18th century we are told that Masons' Lodges formerly met in the open-"on the highest hill or lowest valley, where never dog barked nor cock crew." Brethren will no doubt have read the interesting article in the "Masonic Record" relating to this state of affairs, but I am bound to say that I do not think that the ordinary mediaeval lodge met in such places. The reference to the cock, together with certain details we possess with regard to those lodges which did meet in the open, (they were mostly in Scotland) indicate that they were not ordinary Craft lodges, but much more probably Templar Lodges. The Templars in the 18th century claimed to be descended from a body which had been suppressed in the years 1307 to 1314-, and actually prescribed. There was every reason therefore why they should meet in out of the way places, but no such reason existed in the case of a lodge of ordinary Freemasons. That such a phrase should have wandered into a craft ritual from Templary is perfectly natural, but it is not safe to argue from this that all Masonic lodges met under the canopy of heaven. In those early days, many higher degrees were worked in ordinary Craft Lodges, in a way not permitted to-day; and this may easily account for phrases more appropriate to a Templar Preceptory being found in a Craft working. I might add that until the middle of the 19th century Templar meetings were always called "Encampments," indicating that they were camps held in the open fields. But in mediaeval times we know that the Freemasons had Lodge buildings, and if they went to a new place to build a church or castle , the first thing they did was to erect a temporary Lodge room, which they attended before starting the day's work. Those interested will find abundant details in Fort Newton's interesting little book, "The Builders." There also it is clearly shown that there were two kinds of masons in those days, and the man who conclusively proved this was not a modern Speculative Freemason.

The two groups were the Freemasons and the Guild Masons.

The former were lineal descendants of the Comacine Masons-who, incidentally, knew a certain Masonic Sign-and these men were skilled architects, free to go anywhere. They had a monopoly of ecclesiastical building and of work outside the towns, e.g. castles.

The Guild Masons were humbler folk. They were not allowed to build outside their particular city, but had a monopoly of all building inside that city, with one important and significant exception:-they were not allowed to build ecclesiastical buildings. In return for their charter they had to maintain the fortifications.

When a church had to be built the Freemasons were sent for, and apparently they called on the Guild Masons to help them with the rough work, e.g., to square the stones, etc.

I suggest that Speculative Freemasonry is mainly descended from the Freemasons, whereas the few Operative Lodges that survive are probably descended from the Guild masons.

This theory is borne out by the fact that while the Operatives have our g.s. they have not our s.ns, yet these s.ns are unquestionably old.

They would all have the same g. for convenience in proving to the Freemasons that they were really masons, but they would keep their s.ns to themselves, as did the Freemasons, since they did not want the other group to have access to their private meetings.

Further, we find that the Master Masons of the Freemasons were entitled to maintenance as "gentlemen," clearly indicating that they were different from ordinary craftsmen (See Fort Newton). After the Reformation no doubt Freemasons and Guild masons tended to amalgamate, and this explains much.

Now if the Freemasons erected a lodge before they started to build a church or castle, we shall see that their meeting in the open would be merely occasional, e.g., while the temporary lodge was being built, and not a regular custom ; but the very fact that is was a temporary building, and open to approach by all and sundry who came to the site of the new edifice, is quite sufficient to explain why they had someone on guard.

Why, however, is he called a Tyler, instead of Sentinel, or some similar name?

There are three explanations, and we can adopt which we please:-

1.   To tile is to cover in; hence the Tyler is one who covers or conceals what is going on in the lodge.

2.   In the old mediaeval Templar ceremony there were three sentinels; one inside the door, one outside, and one on the roof or tiles, who could see if anyone was approaching the building. It will be remembered that the old Templar Churches were round, so that a man perched on the roof was able to see in every direction.

3.   That the tilers were inferior craftsmen as compared with the genuine Freemasons; poor brethren, as it were, and not admitted to full membership, although one or two were chosen to act as Outer Guards.

I am not greatly impressed with the latter theory, and my person predilection is in favor of No. 1 ; but there is a good deal to be said for No. 2. The tyler guarded the brethren from "cowans" or eavesdroppers.

The former word is still used in the country districts of Lancashire and Westmorland for a dry-dyker, that is, a man who builds rough walls between the different fields, of rough, uncut, and unmortared stones. When I was living in Yorkshire I had a number of fields so surrounded; the stones for which were picked from the hillside, and piled one upon another. No particular skill was needed to build such a wall; I repaired several myself.

In other words, a "Cowan" is one who pretends to be a mason because he works in stone, but is not one. Some fanciful derivations have been suggested from "Cohen," the Jewish priest. I disagree entirely with this view. Why should the Jewish Cohens be more likely to pretend to be Freemasons than any other priests? As the other word is spelt as we spell ours, and means what I have stated, I see no reason to invent this suggestion regarding the Jewish priests, who were always few in number, and in the Middle Ages hardly existed: the Jews were driven out of England by Edward I., and not re-admitted until the time of Cromwell.

"Eavesdroppers" means men who listen under the eaves. The eaves of a primitive or of a mediaeval cottage overhung a considerable distance beyond the walls, and between the roof and the wall was an open space. Through this space the smoke of the fire escaped; the general arrangement being very similar to that found in the tropics. The walls of such a cottage were often only five to six feet high, and thus a man could stand under the eaves in the shadow, hidden from the light of the sun or moon, and both see and hear what was going on inside, without those who were in the lodge knowing he was there.

But the Tyler was on guard outside the door of the Lodge; he was armed with a d..n s..d, and woe betide any eavesdropper he discovered, for our mediaeval brethren undoubtedly interpreted their obligations literally.

Incidentally, I understand that nominally the duty of carrying out the pen. still rests on the shoulders of the Tyler.

With regard to the use of temporary buildings on or near the site of the edifice, it should be noted that during the building of Westminster Abbey there was at least one, if not two, such lodges, and they are mentioned in the records of the Abbey. One seems to have stood on the site of the subsequent nave.

Thus we can see that it was essential that there should be an Outer Guard to keep off intruders, owing to the fact that Lodges were usually held in temporary buildings, often with overhanging eaves and an open space between the top of the walls and the beams which supported the roof.

The word "hele" should, in my opinion, be pronounced "heal," not "hale." The use of "hale" is due to the fact that in the 18th century the words "conceal," and "reveal," were pronounced "concale" and "revale." Since the words obviously were a jingle, I consider it is more correct to-day to pronounce it "heal."

Moreover, the word "hele" means to cover over. You still hear the phrase used, "to hele a cottage," or even a haystack, and the word "Hell" implies the place that is covered over, e.g., in the centre of the earth. "Hele" is connected with "heal"-to cover up, or to close up, a wound-and the meaning therefore is tautological, viz, "to cover up the word." (The Masonic s -t")

The use of the pronunciation "Hale" is to-day most misleading, and is apt to cause a newly initiated Bro. to think he has to "hail" something, or "proclaim it aloud."

The C. is taken in hand by the Tyler, who makes him sign a form to the effect that he is free and of the full age of 21 years.

Why "free?" Well, in mediaeval days he had to bind himself to serve as an apprentice for seven years. Unless he was a free man, his owner might come along and take him away, before he had completed his apprenticeship and, worse still, might extort from him such secrets as he had learnt from the masons. Thus the master might be enabled to set himself up as a free lance, not under the control of the fraternity.

The twenty-one years is, I believe, an 18th century Speculative innovation, aiming at a similar object. I think there is no doubt that usually in the Middle Ages an apprentice was a boy, who placed himself under the control of a Master with his parents' consent. The Master was henceforth in loco parentis.

In the 18th century without some such safeguard (as 21 years) some precocious youth might have joined the fraternity without his father's consent. The father might have been one who disapproved of F.M., and in such a case would probably have not hesitated to exercise his parental authority in the drastic manner at that time in vogue, and so exhort the secrets, which he could then have "exposed."

To-day it is still a very reasonable clause, for it presupposes that man has reached years of discretion and knows what he is about. Any real hardship is removed by the fact the G.L. has power to dispense, which power it constantly uses in the case of the University Lodges at Oxford and Cambridge. I myself was one of those who thus benefited. It is, I believe, still the custom in England that a Lewis, the son of a mason, may be admitted at 18, though the right is seldom claimed; but in some countries, I understand, it is a privilege highly valued, and regularly used by those entitled to it. In masonry a Lewis is a cramp of metal, by which one stone is fastened to another. It is usually some form of a cross, and a whole chapter could be written on its significance, but this casual reference must suffice.

CHAPTER III.

PREPARATION.

The next thing that happens is that the C. is prepared by the Tyler.

This is a very important matter. There seems little doubt that originally candidates were str..d n..d, and even to-day in the U.S.A. C's are left in their sh-s only.

In Burma we changed out of everything into a one-piece pajama suit, a most convenient arrangement.

What we now have is a system by which the parts which have to be b. are made b.

We take our ob. on our L.K., therefore that. K. must be B.. Why? So that our flesh may be in contact with Mother Earth. It is possible that there was a practical as well as a symbolical meaning in this , and also in the case of our deprivation of m..s. In some of the ancient mysteries it has been suggested that a charge of electricity was passed through the C. as he knelt at the altar, either from a battery, or by what is now called magnetism. If any question the use of electricity in those days, I would point out that certain statements of Herodotus, to the effect that the Egyptian priests brought down lightning by means of rods, can best be explained by admitting that they had some rudimentary knowledge of electricity.

The b.b. is in order that the S.I. can be applied. The Scotch ritual, however, says it is to show your sex, but I am inclined to think this is a modern gloss.

Personally, I should not regard this as conclusive proof in itself, for I have seen (when abroad) many well grown girls who had no breasts worth mentioning, while many native men had quite well developed busts. It should always be remembered that this is the degree of birth and we were born n..d..

We are s. s. because we are about to tread on holy ground, just as in the East we wear slippers when entering a mosque. It is probable that the Scotch ritual has preserved a real tradition when it refers to the custom in Israel of removing a shoe, as a witness, when confirming an obligation. Those interested will find the details in Ruth, where Boaz under-takes to marry Ruth.

A.C.T. is placed about his n..

This piece of symbolism is old and world wide.

On a vase found at Chama, in Mexico, several candidates are depicted going through a ceremony very similar, apparently, to a certain degree in M.,* One is being taught a certain sign, and the others stand waiting their turn all have C.T.s with a running noose about their necks. In India this C.T. is the emblem of Yama, the God of Death, with which he snares the souls of men and drags them forth from their bodies. It is carried by - Shiva to indicate his destructive character in relation to human life.

There are in masonry meanings within meanings, and I will therefore indicate a few of those associated with the C.T. , but I shall not do so with all the details upon which I shall touch.

The C.T. is an emblem of Death. It is fastened round the necks of captives as showing that they are at the absolute mercy of their conqueror. Thus the burghesses of Calais had to come before Edward III. in their shirts-note that-with c.T. 's round their necks. They were only saved by the desperate pleading of good Queen Philippa.

But this is the degree of birth. Some come into the world with a caul which may strangle them if not removed, and in any case we are said to be born in original sin and therefore doomed to die.
*See "Freemasonry and the Gods"

Birth, in the very nature of things, means death, and that is why the Hindu's have made Shiva, the Lord of Death, also the Lord of Birth. We ourselves are captives-souls bound by the chains of the flesh-and offenders against the Law of the King of Kings. Further, we come in bondage to sin, seeking to be freed from our bonds by the word of God. The holding of the C.T. , and the dangers entailed, are sufficiently explained to need no further mention just now, though this does not imply there are not inner meanings.

The h.w. is always found in every great initiatory rite. In general, it reminds us that as in the physical world we came out of darkness into light, so in the intellectual, and finally, in the spiritual world. We come into masonry seeking the Light of God's word.

In other language, to try and comprehend through the use of symbols what God really is.

But as the veil of darkness is slightly lifted as we grow in years and our intellect awakens , so it is in the craft, and the first thing we see there is the V.S.L., itself a symbol of Divine inspiration; for without the Divine spark, which speaks from the inmost recesses of the soul, we shall remain in spiritual darkness all our natural life.

The C. is then brought to the door of the L. and challenged, but strange to say, in our ritual there is no p.w.. There was once, I have no doubt, and it is still in use in Scotland, Ireland and U.S.A. Moreover, it is one of the tests there when visiting, and if a man cannot give it he will run a serious risk of being refused admission. Strange to say, we do get it inside the Lodge, though perhaps most brethren do not realize it. It is "The T. of G.R." (sometimes it is "Free and of G.R.," though this is less usual).

But before entering we are deprived of M.. Now, among the Dervishes M. = mineral substances, but we interpret it M . . . 1. It is M . . . 1s!-that is important. "Valuables" is a real, but subsidiary, meaning.

Let us consider this carefully. There is an explanation of why it is done in the lecture,now, alas, seldom read in Lodge-and also, of course, in the questions. These lectures were the real instruction; on them were based the tracing board Lectures, which were pictorial summaries, on which were set certain questions.

Now the lectures (which can be bought at any Masonic furnishers) tell us that at the building of the Temple no metallic implements were used. Why? Because metals came from below. They were the gifts of the Thonic Gods:-the Gods of the Underworld-useful, no doubt, but being gifts of the Gods of the Underworld they were in their very nature evil, and abhorrent to the Gods of Light, whom the white races worshipped. For this reason the Egyptians continued to use stone knives to open the corpse preparatory to embalming it, long after they used metal knives constantly. The holy dead must not be polluted with the gifts of the evil powers. If there is anything in the theory of an electric or magnetic discharge being made at the time when a metal point is applied to the n. 1. b. at the ob. , this would also be a practical reason; the presence of metal might make such a charge dangerous. But the first reason is no doubt the original one, and probably the only one.

The idea that we bring nothing into this world is, of course, likewise obvious; but its full significance is lost in our ritual, although seen in the Irish. There a C. is deprived of metals in the first and in the second degrees. The significance of this will be realized by M.M.'s if they ponder awhile on the meaning of the S.W.'s P.W.- "How hardly shall a rich man enter the kingdom of Heaven." That worldly possessions hamper a man's spiritual progress is proclaimed by every religion in the world which can truly be called great. The Buddhist monk and the mediaeval friar alike agree on this.

Why p.w.s. at all? Here we wander into a strange field, no less than that of old world magic, I think. The C. enters an E. A. Lodge from the outside world. Prior to his entry this Lodge has been opened by a peculiar ceremony: - a ceremony which, in the technical language of magic and the occult, raises the vibrations of those present; thus they are , as it were , raised to a higher key, and force is generated. Now those who have studied such matters know that a body of men who are all concentrating on a particular subject do generate a peculiar, subtle, but powerful force, which has not been accurately defined by science , but is loosely called magnetic. In the old days of phenomenal magic certain words, when uttered in the correct tone, were believed to be in consonance with this "power," like a tuning fork is to a violin. Therefore we give this p.w. to the C. to raise him quickly to the same "power" as the Lodge. But I am afraid I may be getting rather deep for our younger readers. All I need say further is that such p.w.s are universal in the great mystery rites, ancient or modern, and it is not surprising, therefore, that in some rituals we find a P.W. leading to the 1 degree.

CHAPTER IV.

ADMISSION.

Now our C. enters and is received on a S.L.. This signifies many things, one idea lying within the other. It reminds us of the pain we, as distinct from our mothers, suffered when we entered this physical world. It is a test of our courage and obedience. Probably in olden days blood was drawn, as a sacrifice. The Can. comes seeking for knowledge; self-restraint and quiet confidence should mark his bearing.

In all primitive initiatory rites most painful tests are applied, and if the candidate does not bear them with courage he is rejected, and told that henceforth he is to dress as a woman and will be treated with contempt by the men of the tribe.

We note that the instrument is a Latin cross, the age-old symbol of suffering, and this is the only place in the Lodge where the C. sees this cross, (e.g. when it is shown him later) though M.M. 's may realize that there does come a time when he treads the Way of the Cross of suffering.

The use of a Latin Cross as the S.I. is peculiarly significant, for it is associated with pain and the danger of death, and tells us, in symbolic language, that the way of life is the path of suffering, and begins with the threat of death and ends in death itself: but by this hard road we draw nearer to the object of our quest.

Next the C. kneels while the blessing of H. is invoked. This needs no explanation, for he is about to start on The Quest and needs Divine help. But the phrase, "Relying on such sure support, you may safely rise and follow your leader, . . . , for where the name of God is invoked we trust no danger can ensue" seems pointless in Emulation working, for the danger was at the door and is passed. At Leeds, however, they have a working which is, they say, derived from the Old York ritual, and it does explain this passage.

I saw this ceremony at Alfred 306, Leeds. The C. was brought in h-w and bidden to k . . l., and after the prayer, the W.M. said:-

"Mr. Brown it is but fair to tell you of the perilous position in which you are now placed. Before you stand one with a d.s. in his hand, pointed at your n. l.b. , and behind you one holds the end of the c.t. which is about your neck; in this position of difficulty and danger, in whom do you put your trust?"

Answer:-"In God. "

W.M.:-"Right glad am I to see your faith is so well founded; relying, etc."

Here you see the C. is in danger.

Next the C. is taken round with the Sun, for this is the road of life , and in all ancient religions on entering a temple a man had to follow this path. In Burma to

33

this day you are expected to pass round the pagoda in this manner. The words are:-"Brethren in the N.E.S. and W. will take notice. " It is clear therefore that emphasis is laid on the fact that the candidate is following the path of the Sun, for otherwise why not employ the more usual phrase, "North, South, East and West?" Now the Swastika, which may be regarded as the "lost sign" in Freemasonry (+), indicates the path of the Sun and is the emblem of life, whereas the Swastika is the emblem of the life beyond the grave, for, according to ancient symbolism and eschatology, the departed soul went through the underworld the reverse way, just as the Sun was supposed to do, e.g. W.S.E.N. This then, is the road of the Spirits.

Thus the candidate starts on the symbolic

(+) First suggested by Wor. Bro. Sir John Cockburn.

journey of life, and in some of the eighteenth century rituals there is evidence that the way was made hard and difficult, to symbolize the trials and tribulations we meet with in life , particularly if we strive to attain to the Light. This lesson is still taught in certain foreign rituals.

In "Freemasonry and the Ancient Gods" I have discussed the probability of the theory that the Swastika was once used in our Lodges to represent God, as it still is in the operative lodges, and have shown that a square-a-gamma *, the Greek "G," and therefore that the fourfold gamma represents the four letters of the Hebrew alphabet which denote the

34

sacred name of God. I refer again to this point later, and so will content myself with saying that in an operative lodge the Swastika if formed of four gallow-squares, one of which always rests on the open volume of the Bible, while the other three belong to the three Grand Master Masons, and are placed by them on the Bible before opening the Lodge, in such a way as to form a Swastika.

Thus even to-day in the manner of our progress round the L. we are reminded of that ageold symbol, which is found all over the world,
*First suggested by Wor. Bro. Sir John Cockburn.

Representing Life and the Sun, the latter being itself an emblem for God.

The C. is then told to step off with the l. f. f.. Why? Because the Preserver in ancient mythology is always depicted as trampling with his l. f. on the Serpent of Evil. This is so, alike in ancient Egypt, in India and elsewhere.

But some may ask "Why should Horus or Krishna plant his l. f. on the serpent of Evil?" Major Sanderson, who has spent many years in Nyasaland as Medical Officer of Health and has been initiated into several native rites, tells me that among many primitive races there is a superstition that when entering a shed where rice is stored one must enter r. f. first, "so as not to hurt the Spirit who rules over the rice store." The same idea prevails among these people wherever food is stored, and we here get an explanation of "l. f. f.".

When fighting against the Spirit of Evil you do desire to hurt him, and so reverse the superstition, and step off l. f. f.. This is Major Sanderson's view, and I consider it is probably the correct one.

It may also be well to point out that our ceremonies have come in contact, at various periods, with many different religious beliefs, and this fact explains why there are often several meanings attached to certain points in the ritual, all of which may be correct.

The great serpent, Apepi, in Egypt, represents the powers of spiritual evil, e.g. the Devil.
But it also specifically refers to ignorance, as is shown in the Indian legend in which Krishna tramples on the five-headed cobra. The five heads, moreover, also have a reference to our five senses, which in that allegory must be cleansed of every evil thought.

Thus we may consider that the World is represented by the C.T. and H.W., and the brotherhood helps us to free ourselves from them. The Flesh is represented by the f. r. s. , in which we "trample" on the Tau Cross, while the Devil is represented by the snake, of whose existence we are reminded by the warning to "step off with the l. f. f.".

Strictly, the C. should enter the L. in the N. , not in the West. The North is the place of darkness, and at birth we come out of darkness into physical light, and so in the spiritual journey. This is done at Leeds.

36

Out of darkness, Light. But the Light shineth in the darkness and the candidate comprehends it not, for the darkness of gross materialism is upon him until he kneels before the emblem of the divine light, the V.S.L..

The C. is then challenged by the J.W. and the S.W.. The J.D. gives the pass word "Free and of G.R. ," and the Wardens acknowledge its potency and bid him enter (Note "enter,") as if he were outside a door on which he had knocked for admission. This brings to our mind the three regular knocks.

For reasons which cannot be stated here, but which I will deal with more fully later, I suggest that the E.A. knocks remind us that man is Body, Soul and Spirit, and as in this stage of ignorance the Body is as important as the other two, the three knocks are all of equal duration. Lest any misunderstand this, I would argue that in the process of creation the Spirit first comes from God, secondly, clothes itself with a Soul, and finally enters flesh. Thus, the first knock represents the Spirit, seeking God whence it came, the second, the Soul, and the third, the Body.

To understand the full meaning of this passing by the Wardens one needs to consider why the C. is being led round the L.. There are two reasons given-

(1) To show that he is properly prepared.

(2) To show that he is a fit and proper person to be made a mason.

Being made a mason symbolizes the birth of the Christ within, and before anyone can attain to this mystical re-birth he must have progressed some way along the road of evolution, have gained certain experiences, and learned certain lessons. Think again of the P.W., F. and of G.R.! In the earlier stages man is bound in materialism earthly things satisfy, and he is ruled by his physical passions. The C. for masonry has begun to desire more than the material: he has felt the desire for spiritual growth and knowledge, and so has become "free." This is recognized as he passes the J.W , who represents the Material Nature. Next he approaches the S. W. - the representative of the Soul-and with the aid of the P.W. is again bidden to enter. Notice, having passed the material stage, when the Body reigns supreme, the Soul immediately, takes control, and presents the C. to the W.M.-i.e. the Soul calls upon the Divine Spirit of God to give L. to the C.

The reply is significant, but is almost incomprehensible unless one understands the symbolical journey which the C. has just taken, and one is apt to wonder why the questions which follow were not asked at the very beginning of the ceremony. Really they are most important! They constitute the final testing of the C. before he is bidden to advance towards the E. to receive the L. , and enter on the pathway which begins with initiation and ends with God Himself. Also they "are very searching: the C. being required to declare solemnly that he comes seeking knowledge, not because others desire him to do so, nor yet for unworthy motives of personal gain, but because he is prompted from within by a genuine desire to help Humanity. Then follows a hint that the journey upwards is by no means easy, and patience, perseverance, caution and courage are essential if we are to achieve our goal. The C. having replied satisfactorily, the S.W. is given permission to direct the guide to instruct him in the proper method of advancing towards the L.

This is by three squares which symbolize, not only uprightness of life, but also the three letters of the Great Name, Yod, He, Vau; Male, Female, and Variable. In other words, God the Father, Mother, and child; and the fourth square is on the Ped., which gives us the final He, or the complete name of Him we seek,- Jehovah, or J.H.V.H.

But the letter HE (pronounced Hay) is female, and its female aspect is emphasized by the position of the sq. and c.s., which form a lozenge, itself a well known symbol for the Vesica Piscis, as all who study heraldry know; for in heraldry a woman's arms are placed, not on a shield, as are a man's, but on a lozenge.

A great truth is here taught,-that each soul is part of the Divine whole and cannot be separated from the God we seek. The C. is only just about to emerge from the darkness of gross materialism, yet the God he seeks is within him. True He is so veiled that many do not realize His presence, just as hundreds of C's tread out the proper steps without ever realizing their full significance, but those who rise above the material start on the path of return to God, and each stage that they pass as they progress along the path, reveals more fully His Nature and Being.

Notice, the C. only treads three squares,-Yod, He, Vau; Male, Female, Variable; the fourth square needed to complete the whole is on the Ped. This is particularly significant never whilst in the flesh shall we be able fully to comprehend His nature. No finite mind can comprehend the Infinite Deity. It is only after we have left the first initiation long behind, and traveled far, that we can hope to obtain that transcendent knowledge which enables us to understand fully, the Nature and Being of Him Who is the beginning and end of all.

Again comes the reminder that Masonry is free ; entrance to the path can only be gained by those who hear the call from within. No-one is coerced;-even at this late stage the C. is given an opportunity to retire. Thus he is asked if he is willing to take a serious Ob., and on his agreeing to do so, the W.M. directs him to k. on his l. k. etc. It should be noted that the l. side of an individual is usually said to be "Femine," and it is not surprising, therefore that in this, the first and femine degree, the C. is told to k. on his l. k.. Notice the exact position! On the l. k. keeping the r. f. in the f. of a s. Now when you k. on the l. k. you must of necessity form a sq. at that k. , and, if you try it, you will find that you cannot keep the r. f. in the form of a sq. without keeping the r. k. in the form of a sq. also; so once again we get three sq's, with the fourth on the Ped. Thus we get another glimpse of the truth already hinted at, that each soul is part of the Divine whole, and cannot be separated from God. The C. is only just about to emerge from the darkness of ignorance , and yet he is instructed so to k. that by his very attitude, -i.e. by forming three sq.'s with his body (the fourth being on the Ped.) he shows symbolically that the God he seeks is within. Possibly the C. is not conscious of His presence , any more than he realizes the significance of the steps by which he approached the Ped. , or of the posture he assumes as he k's thereat, yet verily God is with him, and within him, and, be the journey short or long, back to God he must return. Once a M. , ever a M. , there is no such thing as straying permanently from the path.

CHAPTER V.

THE OBLIGATION.

Why should there be any ob. ? In all the ancient mysteries an ob. was exacted, and for this reason: - The secret teachings given in these mysteries disclosed an inner meaning, often of a most exalted kind, unsuitable for the general public, who were lacking in education. In the ancient world the external religion, with its worship of many gods, suited the ordinary man in the street, who was incapable of comprehending more advanced spiritual truths. It would have been dangerous, alike to the populace and to the preacher, to have shouted aloud such a doctrine as the essential unity of God, and still more fatal to have attempted to describe His Nature. The danger to the populace was that the preacher might have destroyed their belief in the religious

41

system in which they had been reared, while failing to convert them properly to the new doctrine. For the preacher, the fate of Socrates, and the failure of the so-called heretic King of Egypt-who tried to popularize the worship of the one God, under the symbol of the Atendisk, or disk of the Sun-are sufficient evidence of the risks which would be encountered.

Moreover, these mysteries all purported to teach certain occult secrets, whose diffusion among vicious, or ignorant, men would have been dangerous.

Even in the Middle Ages these dangers were still very real. Any deviation from orthodoxy might have endangered the social fabric of the community, and such an attempt was certain to involve the advocate of new doctrines in a struggle with Church and State which could only have ended at the stake.

Within an oath-bound Society men felt free to speculate and compare their personal standpoints, while to the outside world they continued to conform to orthodoxy. The fate of the Templars must have been an ever present warning to the speculative mind, in the Middle Ages.

In addition, there is little doubt that the building trades, like other Guilds, had important trade secrets, and wished to safeguard these from interlopers. A mediaeval Guild , on the one hand protected the interests of its members, while on the other it trained those members, and inspected and passed their work;

thus protecting the community from deliberate fraud or careless work. Nor must it be forgotten that in a building bad work might involve actual danger to the users of that building. For all these reasons it was right and proper that no one who was not a member of the fraternity should be in possession of its trade secrets.

The ob. is undoubtedly ancient, but its full significance is realized by few.

The penalty is d. , and in the Middle Ages I do not doubt that it would have been enforced, though to-day it is purely symbolical.

Studying it carefully, we note in passing the word "hele," whose meaning has already been explained, - and also that every printed ritual in existence is a clear breach of our Ob. The strict interpretations of this clause is one of the reasons why we cannot expect to find any mediaeval rituals, although the fact that the bulk of the members in those days could not read or write would lessen the temptation to make them.

From a practical point of view, however, the essential object to-day is to prevent anyone who has not been regularly initiated from entering our Lodges and the printed rituals usually does this, for s. ns., w.s. and g.s. are missing and a careful cross-questioning would undoubtedly lead to the discovery of an imposter, even if he could produce a stolen G.L. certificate.

In the altered conditions of the present era our secrecy is more of the nature of privacy, unlike that which prevails in a political secret society, which usually has revolutionary tendencies.

The old penalty has many striking points. It means that the culprit will be sl., and his b. b . . d. in unconsecrated ground. More than that, the ground can never be consecrated, and, according to the beliefs of the middle ages, and also of the 16th, 17th and 18th centuries, the soul of a man so buried could not rest in peace , but would wander up and down in misery till the Judgment Day. Suicides, for a similar reason, were buried at the cross road, and to prevent their bodies being used by vampires a stake was driven through the middle of the body to keep it nailed down. (It should be noted than even in England the p . . . s vary in different localities).

Thus the culprit is not only d. . . . d to d . . . h, but to be a wandering outcast spirit till the day when the Great Judge consigns it to Hell. It is not perhaps a very charitable, or Christian idea, but that is what is meant all the same.

The T. is removed so that he cannot s. on his own behalf at the Judgment Day.

The more effective punishment is, of course , a later "gloss," inserted at a time when; owing to better police supervision, it would have been dangerous to the members of the Order to enforce the ancient py. To-day, in England, it is the only effective penalty, but in some foreign countries d. is still enforced under certain circumstances. In such cases, however, the Lodges are usually strongly political and revolutionary in tendency. But with us it still remains an obvious symbolical meaning.

Immediately after the Ob. the W.M. says, "Having been kept . . . ."etc. We have seen that the C. has already been asked several questions; these have gradually led up to this, the greatest and most important! Now the climax is reached. It is as if the W.M. says, you have declared that you are here of your own free will, not for unworthy motives, but led by an earnest desire for knowledge. Your humility and obedience have been tested, and you are therefore entitled to request the fulfillment of the greatest desire of your heart. The question put at this moment can be answered by no one but the C. , for it is meant to teach him that essential lesson that no appeal for L. is ever made in vain. His answer given, the w.M. says, "Then let . ." etc. Notice the word restored. Mystical rebirth marks the beginning of our journey towards God the Light, of our ascent towards God, but it is a restoration,-a journey back to Him from Whom we came.

Exactly the same procedure is followed in the initiatory rites of the Turkish Dervishes. Among them, however, the incident is followed by a beautiful exposition of the mystical meaning of Light. It is the Divine Light, emblem of God Himself, and of Divine inspiration. It is, moreover, present, not only in the sacred writings, but in every true believer's heart. The light of the sun itself is but a faint similitude of the Divine Light of God's love, through which, and in which, we have our being.

Though not expressed in our ritual , this act has the same inner meaning, as I have explained.

So to the C.L. is restored, and he sees, what? The V.S.L. , the S. and the C.s. The V.S.L. is in a place of honor, because without its divine standard and authority the S. and C.s. placed thereon would be practically meaningless. These latter form a lozenge, which as I have already said , is a well-known symbol for the Vesica Piscis , which represents the female or preservative principle of the Deity, without which we could not exist for a single day, or hope to be preserved from the powers of darkness which threaten us upon our spiritual journey.

Thus the W.M. 's words teach the aspirant that we have a duty to God, ourselves, and our brother men.

The C. is raised with the proper g. , but this is not explained at once. Rather his attention is directed to the three lesser lights, which we are told represent the Sun, Moon and the Master.

As our Lodges are at present arranged the W.M. should point to the S. for the Sun, and to the W. for the Moon , but it must be admitted that the lesson to be derived from these three luminaries is not very clear. Indeed, the Moon plays no real part in our mysteries, which are essentially solar in character, while the implied contrast between Sun, Moon and Master is in no way helpful.

In reality the three lesser lights are the W.M. and his two wardens, with their respective candles, and these officers have a real symbolic meaning of great importance, which symbolic characters they maintain consistently throughout all three degrees.

My personal view is that it was to the lights on the pedestals, and their respective officers, that this phrase originally applied, and that the Sun and Moon are 18th century interpolations.

THE THREE PRINCIPAL OFFICERS

In any case this makes a convenient place in which to consider the symbolic meaning of the three principle officers in a lodge. The W.M. represents the rising Sun, and in this sense he covers two distinct meanings: the first in connection with the nature of God, and the other with regard to the nature of man. And a similar dual character exists in the case of S.W. and J.W..

The W.M. represents God the Creator, He who calls the Lodge into being, He who created the World out of Chaos. In India this aspect of God, the Incomprehensible, has been individualized as Brahma, so that the devotee many be able to comprehend Him, at least in part.

It is the Master who opens the Lodge, who calls it out of nothing. He sits in the East, the place of light; but though he opens, he does not close the lodge. That is the work of another aspect of the Divine Being.

In the nature of man the W.M. represents the Spirit, the Divine Spark within us, ever striving for the light, never truly separated from the divine source of its being. This dual aspect of the W.M. and his principal officers must be borne in mind, if we are to delve down into the inner, or esoteric, meaning of our wonderful rituals.

The S.W. represents the Setting Sun, and hence the Destructive, or Transformative, aspects of the Deity. Among the Hindu's this aspect is called Shiva. He shall one day close the Grand Lodge of this World, when time shall be swallowed up into Eternity. The S.W. closes the Lodge. As the Destroyer he reminds us that Death, the great leveler, will bring all men low, and his symbol is the Level. This in itself reminds us of the caste mark of Shiva, which consists of horizontal lines.

But in the nature of Man he represents the Soul, which alone enables the Spirit to raise the body towards divine things. Without the medium of the Soul, the Spirit would be unable to influence the body. It is for this reason that the C. is invested in craft masonry by the S.W. or Soul, and not by the W.M. , representing the Divine Spark. Thus we learn that we must raise ourselves, step by step , towards the Divine Light. Shiva is, above all, the great M.M..

The J.W. represents the Sun in its Meridian. He stands for the Way of Life, the balance between birth and death. His is the sunny side of life. He calls us from labors to refreshment and from refreshment to labors. In the divine aspect he represents the Preserver, called Vishnu in India, of whom it is stated that as Rama he sent the skilful craftsmen, Hanuman , to build the bridge for Him , by means of which He crossed the straits to fight against the powers of evil in ancient Ceylon.

Vishnu is associated with the element of water and with corn, and his caste mark is a perpendicular, straight line, referring to the rain which falls from heaven. This symbol is remembered in our lodges by the plumb rule.

In the nature of man he stands for the body, which perishes. He is H.A.B. in the Grand Lodge at Jerusalem. He represents the life and sufferings of the body, only terminated by death; the body which in every man dies before its divine work is accomplished. Our divine temple is not finished at death: all that we can hope is that the foundations have been well and truly laid. In short, in this life we cannot hope to "see God face to face," nor, being finite, can we truly comprehend the Infinite, but we can hope to make such progress that, when called hence, we shall be able to continue , and complete , the work of our own salvation on the foundations of a good and spiritual earthly life.

Finally, it will be noted that in every degree these three officers co-operate to advance the C., and so it is in the spiritual life, for body, soul and spirit' must co-operate if real progress is to be attained.

49

Next the C. is informed of the three great dangers-note the triplicity again-and the few sentences devoted to them must be considered in the light of what has already been written by me on the S.I., the C.T., and the Ob..

At the door of the L. the C. was in great danger, because entrance thereat marked the beginning of the ceremony of initiation into m., and initiation symbolizes the mystical rebirth, the end of the descent into matter and the beginning of the ascent to God, and there can be no more critical time than that. The S.I. warns us of the dangers of rushing unprepared into the field of occultism, while the C.T. indicates the danger that the Divine Spark may be quenched, strangled by materialism, if we do not continue steadfastly. But even when these dangers are passed, throughout the whole of our mystic journey there remains that last danger of our ob., namely, that of infidelity to the vows which marked our entrance, or of abandoning our further quest for light;-knowing the right, but deliberately choosing the wrong. This means death; not primarily physical death, but that greater death, referred to by our Hindu Brethren as "Being born again at the bottom of the ladder of evolution up which we have for so long been ascending. "

We next come to the moment, so long expected, when the s. . . . s are disclosed. No doubt many Brethren could not suppress a slight feeling of disappointment at their comparative insignificance. Was such a tremendous Ob. necessary to safeguard a S. , W. , and G. which appear to be Purely arbitrary?

This question is a fair one, and the answer is that the Ob. safeguards, not so much the G., etc., which are but the outward and visible signs, as the inner esoteric meaning, hidden in our ritual, and never properly explained.

Firstly, the W.M. instructs the C. in the f. r. s., which on investigation proves to be the tau cross.

The tau cross was originally the phallus, and has many inner meanings. It is the emblem of generation and creation, but since these powers may be prostituted they must be brought under control. As the f. r. s. , it represents our natural and animal passions, which must be trampled underfoot and brought under complete control, otherwise we cannot make any advancement in Freemasonry. In plain language, unless we bring our passions into complete subjection, we cannot hope to advance towards a true knowledge of God. For that, I consider, is the real search, or quest, in Freemasonry.

Therefore in every one of the Craft degrees we trample on the tau cross. It will be remembered that one of the charges against the Templars, in 1307, was that they trampled on the cross, and this charge seems to be correct. Yet these same men adored the Cross three times a year in their ceremonies and, moreover, fought and died for it on many a corpse-strewn field in Palestine.

I have no doubt this act of theirs was a symbolic one , associated more with the cross as an emblem of our passions than with the Christian cross of suffering.

Yet symbols emerge by imperceptible degrees into each other, and so it is that we can truly say that Christ was crucified on the Cross of our passions. In mediaeval pictures you will usually find that while Christ hangs on a Latin, or four armed cross, the two thieves are hung on Tau , or three-armed crosses. This indicates that they died for their own sins, but Christ, Who hangs on the cross of sacrifice, died for the sins of others.

Thus, my brothers, the f. r. s. is full of inner meaning nor is this the only place in which we meet with the tau cross in the craft. Its higher and holier aspect when associated with the W.M. I shall discuss later.

CHAPTER VI.

CONCLUSION OF THE CEREMONY

Having taken the f. r. s. the C. is given the S.. This he is told refers to the P. of his Ob., and no doubt it does, but it also seems to refer to something much more startling. The part of the body indicated has always been regarded as an important occult centre. In some strange way, the laws of which are but little understood, it has always been associated with the phenomena known amongst psychic students as Materializations. As, however, this subject lies somewhat outside our theme, we will discuss the point no further.

But all our P. 's have a striking analogy to the legend of the creation of man as given by the Hindu sages. From Brahma sprang all four castes. From His head came the Brahmins, from His Breasts the Kshatra, or fighting caste, from His Belly, the peasants, and from His feet, the Sudras. The latter were not true Arians, and were not twice born men; in other words, only the first three castes were regarded as really and truly admissible to the Temple of the High Gods, and free to participate in Their worship.

It will be noted that in this degree the S..n suggests the cutting off of the first caste from those below. This S..n, Bro. Major Sanderson suggests, was originally a mantra, or magic prayer, which must be most carefully guarded from the profane.

The T. appears to be an arbitrary one, although it may possibly refer to a certain pillar. Explanations of this, together with the meaning, derivation, and significance of the W., are reserved for the next volume, for reasons which will be obvious to those entitled to know them.

No doubt, however, the basic idea of both pillar and word is phallic, and other interpretations have evolved later.

Having received s. w. and t. , the C. is warned to be cautious and told how to receive a challenge, then, having been given strength to help him on his way, he is sent forth in order that the important lesson of caution may be implanted in his mind.

The testing by J.W. and S.W. are obviously of practical use, but I think that here also there is an inner meaning. The Body and Soul test the Cand. to see that the lessons have been well and truly learnt; also there seems to be a definite astrological reference.

Having satisfied these important officers, the s.w. asks for some special mark of favor. That is, the Soul calls on the Spirit, but is told that it is the Soul which must invest the regenerate man with the outward signs of the change he has undergone. This point has already been mentioned, but its deep significance must not be forgotten. It may truly be said that it is the S.W. who sets the seal on the candidate's initiation, and proclaims him as at length a member of the Order.

The address of the S.W. and the subsequent one by the Master, are fairly self-explanatory. But one or two points deserve stressing.

The reference to the antiquity of the apron refers mainly, of course, to its use among the Operatives, and implies the dignity of honest labors. The present form of our apron is comparatively modern, but there is evidence that our predecessors, the Comacine Masons , wore aprons when they met in Lodge , and aprons have had a special significance among many religious systems. Thus some of the Chinese gods wear aprons, and I have a photograph of one (See The Hung Society, Vol. III., op. p. 122) and this "God" is making a certain high degree sign. Among the ancient races of America the apron was also evidently used with a religious significance (see picture of the Toltec Preserver in "Freemasonry and the Ancient Gods").

The address of the W.M. lays stress on the importance of not entering the L. if a brother is at variance with another. At first sight this may seem a somewhat unnecessary charge. Normal, well conducted gentlemen are not likely to start an unseemly wrangle in Lodge , even if they are at enmity; and should two men so far forget the common decencies of life as to do so, the W.M. has ample power to deal with the situation.

The real significance of the injunction, however, is that it implies that the mere presence of two brethren who are at variance will disturb the harmonious atmosphere of the meeting. This is a purely spiritual atmosphere, and the belief that such disturbance would occur without any open disagreement, is correct.

In short, such differences disturb the spiritual atmosphere, prevent concentration, and can be detected by sensitive individuals.

Every Lodge has an "atmosphere of its own," and any sensitive man who comes to it can detect it* I have myself noticed the different "atmospheres" of various lodges, and also variations in that of my own.

Too much regard therefore cannot be paid to this rule, and if ignored the Lodge will certainly suffer.

The C. is placed in the N.E. corner of the Lodge for the reason given in the ritual, but it is important to remember that he himself is building his own temple- a spiritual temple to the glory of God.

Why should the cornerstone be laid in the N.E.? This was for a very practical reason; namely, so that the Operatives could work round with the Sun, and thus obtain the maximum amount of light. Symbolically, it refers, of course, to the journey of the soul, which begins in the N., enters life at the East, at birth, and so proceeds to the West, where death ends our day.

The position in which the C. stands is not only a sq., the emblem of rectitude and of God, but at the particular point he make a "Lewis," or angle clamp, which binds together the life which has been (in the North) and his future life (in the East). In physical life the North is pre-natal, but in the spiritual it is before we turned to better things. Above all, such a clamp gives rigidity and strength to the corners, and assures stability. It will be noted that this position in like manner makes a "footing stone."

The testing of the candidate is explained, but perhaps I ought once more to remind my reader that it is absolutely essential that we should leave behind us the baleful gifts of the underworld and the canker of wealth, which destroy spirituality.

The lecture on the working tools explains itself. It appears to be mainly 18th century work.

CHAPTER VII.

THE CHARGE

When the C. has been restored to his personal comfort he receives the charge. The first significant point is the phrase "Ancient, no doubt it is, as having subsisted from time immemorial." In "Freemasonry and the Ancient Gods" I have endeavored to show that this phrase is literally true , and a strong claim can be made that modern Freemasonry is the lineal descendant of the Ancient Mysteries, via the Roman Colleges of Architects, the Comacine Masons, and the Mediaeval Freemasons.

The other significant phrase is that relating to "The Ancient Landmarks." Much learned discussion has taken place concerning what these are. Common sense indicates the following points as obviously falling within this heading, whereas many others may be matters of opinion, on which brethren are entitled to differ.

1.-The signs, words and tokens. If these were changed it would shatter the universality of Freemasonry and prevent old masons recognizing new ones, or members of various jurisdictions doing so. It must be acknowledged that the charge mad by the Ancients against the Moderns, that they had removed the Ancient Landmarks, was largely justified, for they appear to have transposed the w.s. in the first and second degrees. Still apparently, they did not entirely change them.

2 & 3.-Belief in God and a Future Life. I these are removed, then the object and purpose of masonry is destroyed, since it is the "quest of knowledge of, and union with, God." Again, the elimination of the idea of a future life" would destroy the teaching of one of the most important craft degrees.

If these landmarks were removed, Freemasonry would either perish, or else have to substitute a new object, as the Grand Orient of France has done. This having become atheistical, had to turn masonry into a secret political society, with disastrous results.

Hence it is that the Grand Lodge of England felt compelled to break off fraternal relations with that body.

4.-The Order of the Degrees. If these were reversed or changed it would reduce the whole system to nonsense.

The remainder of this address is fairly clear as it stands. It contains excellent teaching, the meaning of which lies on the surface, and so we need spend no further space on it here.

The first tracing board contains a great deal of useful instruction, but it is so seldom given in most lodges that we will pass it by, hoping at some future date to give it the attention it deserves.

The purpose of these tracing boards will be explained in the book dealing with the second degree, and we can therefore take leave of the Entered Apprentice. There is no pretense that we have exhausted the subject, much more could be written, but in a small book like this the author must restrict himself to giving an outline explanation, and suggestions for study, in the hope that his readers will follow the hints given, and discover further meanings for themselves.

CHAPTER VIII

THE CLOSING OF THE FIRST DEGREE.

The first degree closing is remarkably short, and its meaning is fairly clear. The candidate has not yet advanced sufficiently far to be able to appreciate any more esoteric teaching. He is therefore given one brief and tremendous lesson. The Destructive side of the Deity is invoked, and the same officer, it must be remembered, also represents the Soul.

Thus, at the very beginning of his symbolical career, the novice is warned of the inevitable end. During the ceremony of his initiation the fact has been impressed upon him that his spiritual advancement is by means of his soul, i.e. when the S.W. invests him with his apron. Now he is warned that the same soul which may help him to rise, may also cause his spiritual destruction. But even more this fact should show him that, when he has learned all that life can teach him, the Soul acting on the instructions of God, calls him to other fields of usefulness.

It should also be noted that the S.W. closes in the name of the G.A., and by command of the W.M. , thus reminding us of Alpha and Omega, the Beginning and the End.

CONCLUSION.

This then concludes our consideration of the meaning of the first degree. The author has not tried to be exhaustive, and would stress the point that usually he has only attempted to give one esoteric meaning, although often there are other inner meanings, each within the other. But he trusts he will have helped his brethren to perceive that there are indeed deep and invaluable meanings hidden within our ritual, and that his readers, having once started on this line of study, will not rest content until they themselves have discovered further inner meanings. If this be so, then this little book will not have been in vain.

The Biography of
J.S M. Ward

John Sebastian Marlowe Ward was born on 22ndDecember 1885 in
what is now known as Belize City, Honduras and died on July 2nd, 1949
near Limassol Cyprus

His father, the Reverend Herbert M. Ward was an Anglican priest serving the
English community in British Honduras, when his first son, John, was born, but
was recalled to England late in 1888, after which he took up a new post as curate
of St Mary's Church, London. John and his younger brother Reginald, grew up
in London where the boys attended the Merchant Taylor's School. The brothers
were close and within the family John was always known as "Jack" and
Reginald as "Rex". In this article, however, we will continue to call John Ward,
"John", the name by which he was known to the world.

John had extremely poor eyesight and wore thick glasses from a very young
age, but he was bright and went on to Trinity College Cambridge. There at the
age of nineteen, he married his second cousin Caroline Lanchester who was
several years older than he and by whom he had a daughter, Blanche. He
graduated with honours from Cambridge in 1908, majoring in History, and his
first book, a short history of "Brasses" was published at about the same time.
He commenced work as a teacher and also began to write about History and
Freemasonry, in which he had always been interested.

Over the next twenty years he was to produce a large number of books on the
history and spiritual meanings of Freemasonry. He also wrote for various
journals and became a contributor to the Encyclopaedia Britannica on several
subjects, and remained listed as such till long after his death.

His Masonic books discuss not only the Western forms of Freemasonry, but
various other similar secret societies both past and present in different parts of
the world. Most of these books are still in print and many are still regarded as
authoritative by modern Freemasons almost a century after they were first
written. There are literally hundreds of references to J.S.M. Ward and his
Masonic books on the internet.

61

John Ward's career as a Freemason was an illustrious one, but it was merely a passing phase in the journey of his life. He had always been interested in many other subjects, particularly history, religion and science, but a completely new dimension was added to his researches early in 1914. On 5th January 1914 his uncle and grand father-in-law, Herbert J. Lanchester died unexpectedly and a week later John had a dream that was to introduce him to the then "way-out" world of spiritualism.

He recorded these early psychic experiences in his first psychic book, Gone West, which was published a few years later. In it he describes how he met his uncle in the Realms Beyond, and then for more than six months made regular contact with him on the Spirit Plane. When his younger brother Rex, a lieutenant in the York and Lancaster Regiment, was killed in Flanders on Good Friday, 1916, John Ward deliberately set out to contact him in the Afterlife. The success of his efforts is described in a second Psychic book entitled a Subaltern in Spirit Land.

With the outbreak of the First World War, Ward, unable to enlist because of his eyesight was sent out to Rangoon, Burma as the headmaster of the Diocesan Boys School – an Anglican secondary school that provided free education for the Eurasian boys of Burma. At that time there were many such schools in Burma and John Ward, by virtue of his position wrote to Lord Kitchener, the head of the British Army, offering to raise a brigade of troops from among the Eurasian boys in those schools. Kitchener's reply was abrupt and abrasive. "England has no need of half-castes" was the gist of it and so Ward's grandiose plan was summarily dismissed, late in 1914. A year later, with England desperate for soldiers, the army asked Ward to revive it, but not surprisingly the resentment caused by the first rejection meant that most of the Burmese "half-castes" were no longer willing to fight for Britain. Ward persuaded a number of boys from his own school to enlist, but they were far fewer than the full Brigade he had originally proposed to raise.

Whilst in the Far East, Ward spent time in Ceylon and India as well as Burma. He took this opportunity to continue his researches into the spiritual and, perhaps most importantly, received ordination as a Brahmin High Priest, in the Madura Temple in southern India. This, together with his studies of the Chinese

62

Hung Society, led him to take a further interest in spiritualism and theosophy when he returned to England. This happened early in 1916 for health reasons. Ward's health had never been good and since moving to Burma, his digestion had suffered significantly. It was only later that he discovered that this was because his servant had been trying to kill him by mixing ground glass with his food. Although he recovered in England, his digestion caused him problems for the rest of his life. Soon after his return to England, his brother Rex (Reginald L. Ward) was killed in an artilery attack in Flanders, and John Ward spent some time assisting him to become established in his new life beyond the grave. Shortly afterwards, their mother, Alice Ward (nee Carver) died, and the two boys were also able to help her become established on the Astral Plane.

In 1918, John Ward obtained employment with the Federation of British Industry and remained with them until 1930, by which time he had become head of the Intelligence Department - that is to say that he was responsible for assessing business opportunities around the world and making recommendations to British Investors. As the Great Depression, was then wracking the land, no one could understand why he resigned in 1930, but to him there was a very good reason.

In 1918 he had commenced to take an interest in the Theosophical movement, but continued his links with various Masonic groups and writing his books. After publishing his second Spiritualist work he also continued to develop his experience in this field, but through his father, who was still the Vicar of St Mary's, John retained his link with Christianity and remained a member of the Anglican Church until it rejected him in 1934.

In the experiences described in his first two Psychic books, Ward had explored the two Planes of Existence closest to the Physical – generally known as the Astral Plane and the Spirit Plane. He had done this with the help of a number of different inhabitants of each Plane but found that whilst each of these Planes contains many sub-divisions, beyond them there exist many still higher Planes of Being. These correspond to what Christians call the Realms of Saints and Angels, but Ward realised that he as a mere mortal could not hope to reach them. This perhaps more than anything else contributed to the upgrading of his spiritual seeking, which began in the first part of the 1920's.

It was during this period of his life that his wife suffered from a debilitating mental disease which eventually killed her in 1926. It was also during this period that he first met his second wife Jessie Page, with whom he was later to assail the heights of mysticism.

Many people do not understand the difference between a psychic and a mystic, and of course the subject is a large one, but basically a psychic is restricted to experiences linked with the Realms of Man – the Physical, Astral and Spirit Planes. A mystic may be a psychic, though he/she is not always one, but a mystic differs from a psychic in that he/she can travel beyond the Realms of Man. This is achieved only through the help and guidance of a Higher Being - a Saint or Angel, or perhaps even God Himself. This, of course is comparatively rare, and especially in great mystics, there is always the danger of self-deception. There are a a number of key tests that must be applied to eliminate this possibility

One may dream that one has met a dead person, or received some sort of psychic communication from him/her but how does one prove to a cynic that the experience was real and not just the product of one's imagination? There are, of course a number of ways, but perhaps the most convincing test, comes when one dreams of another living person, who, when asked is also able to report basically the same experience. When one is a mystic, having experiences on Higher Planes, such confirmation is extremely rare, but it was just this sort of confirmation that led John and Jessie Ward to realise that their experiences were real – not just the product of an over-active imagination

For the Wards, the first such experience came in 1927, when they both dreamt that they were summoned into the presence of a great Angel, told that Christ was about to begin His Descent through the Celestial Planes to the Earth and asked to help in the Preparation for His Coming. This great Angel, of the order of the Thrones, was to become their constant Guide and helper in the years ahead.

Needless to say they both agreed to dedicate the remainder of their lives to this task. On waking their resolve was further strengthened by the discovery that not only did both remember the same experience, but also that each had recalled details that the other had forgotten, and yet when reminded thereof, the second could not only recall it, but could further extend the narrative.

They married soon after and still in 1927, John gave a series of lectures, in which he explained his discoveries and his new calling. From those who came to listen he gained a few followers and the whole group pooled its resources. They purchased a large house in Barnet on the outskirts of London and then built a church on the property, which was also adorned with many antiques and works of art. In 1930, John Ward resigned from his job at the Federation of British Industry and with the help of his community established the country's first Folk Park.

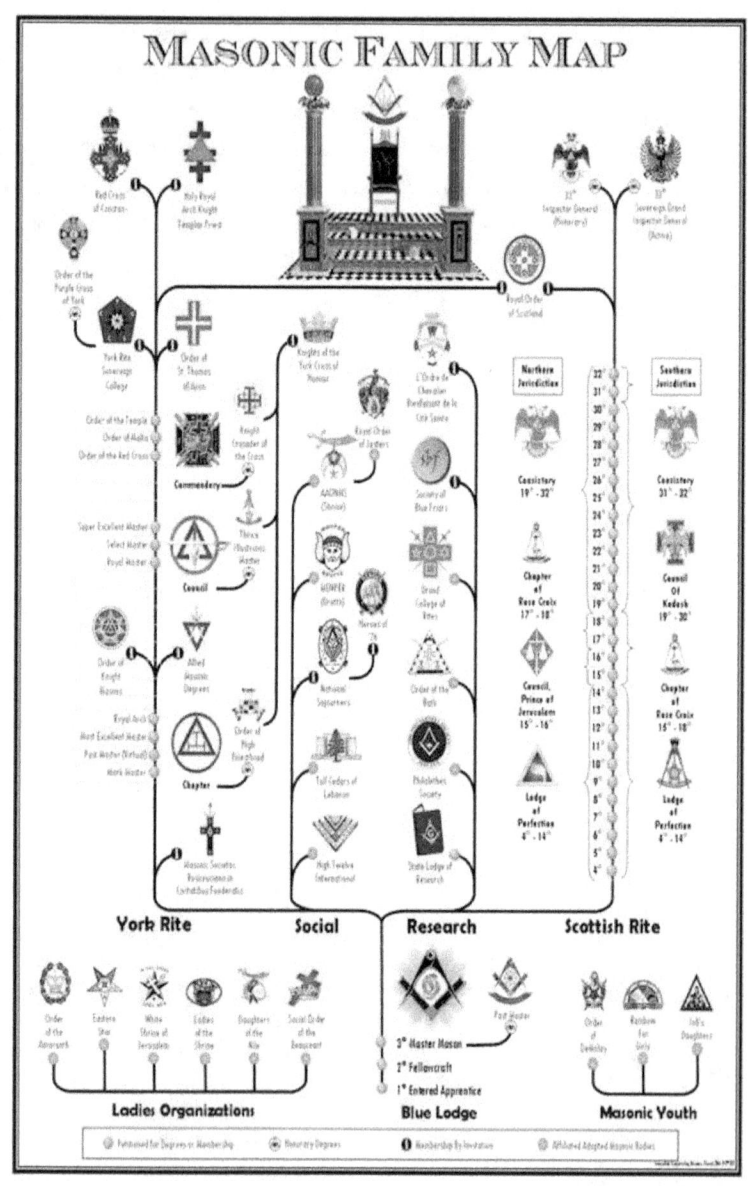